Tin punch pattern used in Five-Drawer Chest (page 28) and Punched Pie Pan Grapevine Wreath (page 37).

SOURCES

Folk Art acrylic colors by Plaid Enterprises, Inc.
Golden Taklon synthetic brushes by Loew-Cornell, Inc.
Graphics by Kathy Shaw
Five-Drawer Chest from Treasures, Lakeview, OH

The patterns for the other projects in this book are full size. Your local craft store may obtain pieces from the manufacturer or from distributors of decorative painting supplies. For a list of manufacturers and distributors, send a self-addressed stamped envelope to:

The Golden Goose Project List
Decorative Design Studio, Inc.
Route 3, Box 155
Smithsburg, MD 21783

Follow me!

GENERAL SUPPLIES

BRUSHES

In decorative painting, good quality **art brushes** are your most important tools. To try to work with poor or improperly cared for brushes is frustrating and unrewarding. I prefer to work with Loew-Cornell Series 7550 Flat, size ½"; Series 7300 Shaders, sizes 2, 4, 8, and 12; Series 7000 Round, size 4 and the specially designed Jackie's Liner, Series JS, size 2. Loew-Cornell has packed these brushes into the kit shown in Figure 1. Although additional sizes are used in the book, these brushes provide an adaptable range of sizes from narrow to wide, suitable for getting started. Once you are hooked on decorative painting you will want to add other sizes within the series.

The **surface preparation brushes** shown in Figure 2 include Loew-Cornell Series 7550 1½" wash brush, a large mop brush, and two foam or poly brushes, 1½" and 1". The straight edge brushes are used for applying sealer, basecoat paints, and varnish. The round edge mop brush is used in antiquing. Although the foam brushes are inexpensive and disposable, I prefer the 7550 wash brush. It facilitates surface preparation, getting into tight places easily, and painting clean, even edges. It is more expensive initially, but, in addition to appreciating its quality, I find myself taking better care of it, so it far outlasts countless foam brushes.

PAINTS, PALETTE, PALETTE KNIFE, BRUSH WASHER

The **paints** featured in this book are Plaid Folk Art acrylics. The **palette** is a surface upon which paints are placed for intermixing and for loading into the brushes. For acrylics, a waxed surface is preferable as it is does not crinkle under the waterbased paint. Disposable palettes (such as the one shown in Figure 3), consist of a pad of tear-off sheets. Other items which serve well as palettes include plastic meat trays, a piece of glass with edges taped for safety, or a white porcelain dish. The latter items may be easily cleaned by soaking in water for a half hour or so. Any dried acrylic is then quickly peeled off.

The **palette knife** is used for mixing colors together. It is also used for patching flaws and filling holes in projects with wood filler. The **brush washer** contains water for cleaning acrylic paints from brushes. A jar can serve this purpose equally well.

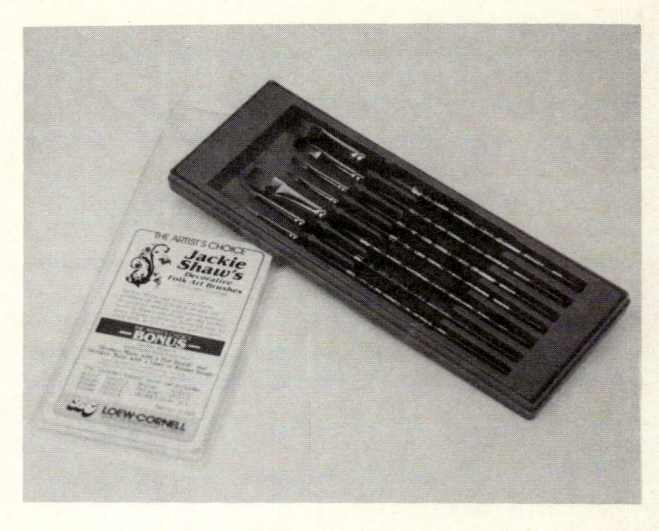

Figure 1. Jackie Shaw's Decorative Folk Art Brush Kit

Figure 2. Surface preparation brushes

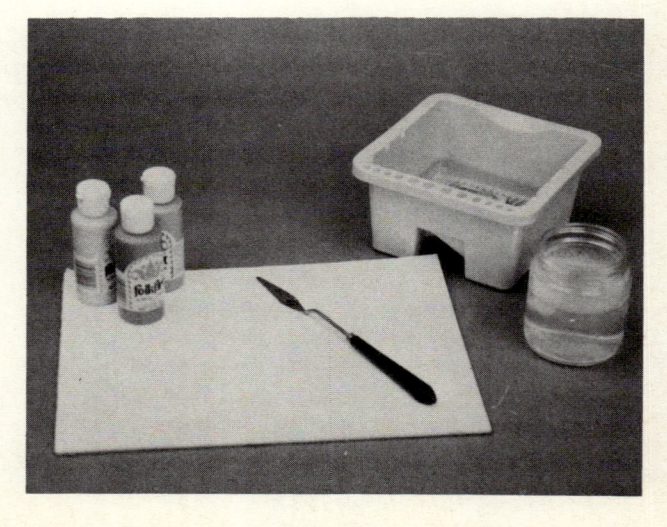

Figure 3. Paints, palette, palette knife and brush washer

TRACING PAPER, CHALK, CHALK PENCIL

Tracing paper is used for copying designs and transferring them onto projects. It is also useful for practicing brush strokes on. The **chalk** and **chalk pencil** are used in designing and transferring patterns. See Figure 4.

SURFACE PREPARATION SUPPLIES

Woodfiller (or powdered wood putty) is mixed with water and used for filling holes and flaws in wooden projects. **Sandpaper** is necessary to smooth the grain and prepare it for the sealer. **Sealers,** such as sanding wood sealers, waterbase varnish, or shellac seal the wood. Clear shellac is preferable, as it also prevents sap and knots in wood from staining through basecoats of paint and spoiling the decoration. These supplies, shown in Figure 5, are available in hardware stores.

The **Home and Hobby Pad** and **abrasive sponge** shown are also ideal for smoothing fine dust. **Cheesecloth** (also found in the food preserving section of your grocery store and in some craft and variety stores) is used in antiquing and for some special effects.

MISCELLANEOUS SUPPLIES

Other supplies you will find helpful are paper towels, stylus, bottle caps or 35mm film lids, plastic wrap, natural sponge, jars, Ivory soap, cotton swabs, linseed oil or finishing oil, notebook for saving your practice sheets, Purex cleaning pads (an abrasive sponge that can be used for sanding—found in the grocery store near SOS pads and scouring powders), drafting tape, glues (such as Tacky, Dow-Corning Rubber Silicone Clear Adhesive, hot glue), Wrico pen (for striping).

Figure 4. Tracing paper, chalk, and chalk pencil

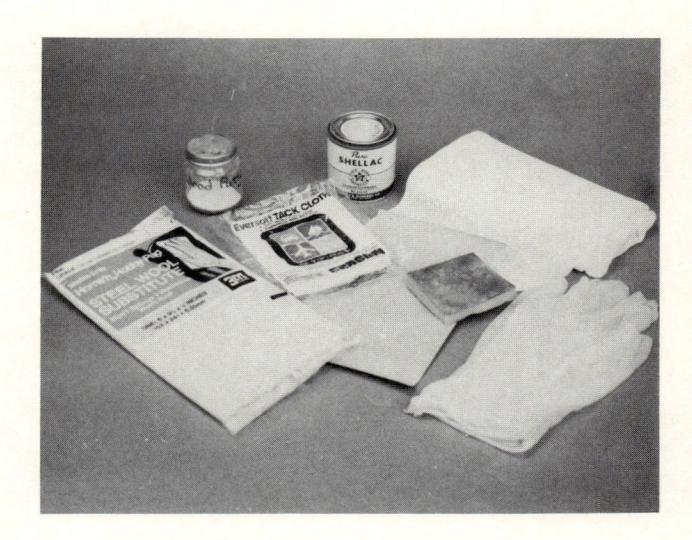

Figure 5. Surface preparation materials

ARRANGING YOUR WORK AREA FOR CONVENIENCE AND COMFORT

Find a layout for your supplies which is the most convenient and which requires the least expenditure of effort. For instance, paper towels for blotting wet brushes should be close to the water and near your painting hand. If you're right handed, your brushes should be close to your right hand, not halfway across the table out of easy reach. Access to the paints on your palette should be unobstructed. Some artists, particularly when working with a limited palette (only a few paints), always squeeze the colors onto their palette in the same order, so that their movements are automatic; not a moment is wasted looking around for a certain color. My favorite arrangement is shown in Figure 6.

An extra jar of water is handy for acrylic painters to have nearby. Use this water for washing soap out of brushes. It is desirable that soap not contaminate your rinse water as it diminishes the adhesive quality of the acrylics.

See that you are comfortably seated at your work area. Some painters prefer sitting on a high stool, others opt for a comfortable chair. If you are working on your project on the work table, be sure you are at a height which does not require you to raise your shoulders to work. Otherwise, you will tire quickly. In such a case, push your chair away from the table and hold the project in your lap, letting your arms hang freely by your sides.

Take mini breaks from time to time. A two-hour session is generally long enough to persevere at painting. Give yourself a stretch break for a few minutes. When you return to your painting, you will have a fresh perspective and renewed vigor. By taking refreshing little breaks, you should be able to continue painting day and night. This devotion to your new hobby gives the dust bunnies plenty of time to multiply, undisturbed in the corners. Children will outgrow clothing without

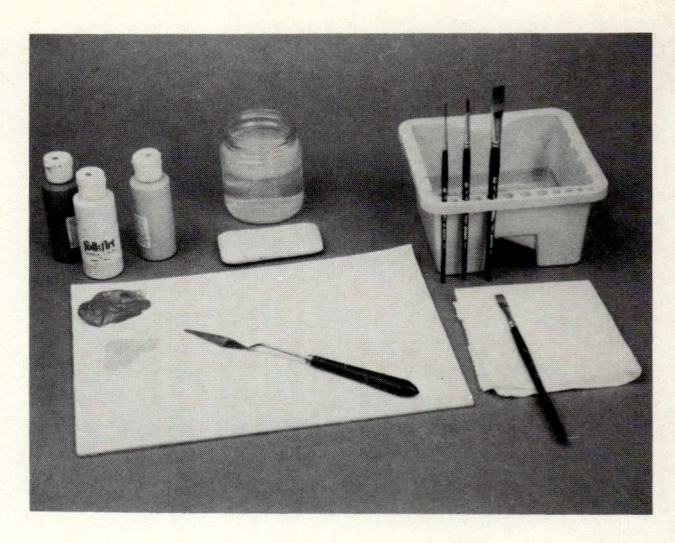

Figure 6. An example of a painting area comfortably arranged for a right handed person. "Lefties" should simply reverse the arrangement.

your ever having to mend or iron. Spouses will learn culinary and laundry skills in order to get from one day to the next. And all the money saved by resorting to quick, unimaginative meals can be stashed away to purchase more painting supplies.

KEEPING YOUR ACRYLICS FRESH LONGER

While acrylics lend themselves so beautifully to decorative folk painting because of their rapid drying time, that very feature can be a bit frustrating when they dry out on your palette while you are still trying to work with them. This is particularly true of combinations of colors which you have worked laboriously to mix. It is possible to prolong their palette life by following the steps below. See Figure 7.

1. Scrape paints into a compact pile and cover with a small cap. I have found 35mm film container lids to be ideal. Once pressed down onto the palette, they seal tightly, preserving the paint under them for several hours. If you expect to be away from your palette for a long time, sprinkle a drop or two of water over the pile of paint before covering it.
2. Mist water over your palette with an atomizer or spray bottle (such as those containing window cleaner or hair spray).
3. Use a styrofoam meat tray or other tray with raised sides, as your palette. Keep it covered with a damp paper towel. If you are using the stiffer tubed acrylics, squeeze them directly onto a damp paper towel, or onto a specially made palette, the Sta-Wet Palette by Masterson.

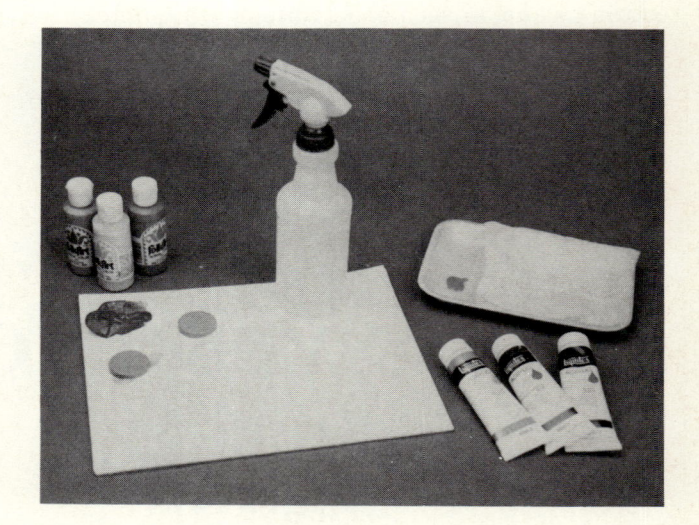

Figure 7. Materials for keeping acrylics fresh on the palette.

CARE AND HANDLING OF BRUSHES

Your brushes represent a good investment. Treat them with care and respect, and they will work better for you and last longer.

1. Clean your brushes often and thoroughly. A quick swish through the water is **not** enough. Use Ivory soap and your fingers to gently work the soap into the hairs as shown in Figure 8. Rinse. Continue soaping and rinsing until every trace of color is gone! Paint allowed to harden in your brush, even in minute amounts, eventually creates a hard "knot" up near the metal ferrule. This "knot" causes the hairs to separate and thereby reduces the effectiveness of the brush. A brush thus damaged can sometimes be partially restored by cleaning with a solvent such as nail polish remover or alcohol. This is a harsh measure, so should be resorted to only when absolutely necessary. Keep solvent away from the handle as it will penetrate the lacquer and create a very sticky situation.

2. After thoroughly cleaning the brush, put more soap into it and reshape the hairs as shown in Figure 9. Shape round and liner brush hairs to a fine point. Shape flat brushes to a smooth chisel edge. Dry. The hairs should be quite stiff. This helps them to retain their crisp shapes, and minimizes damage in storage.

3. Store the brushes so the hairs will not be bent or crushed. Some possibilities shown in Figure 10 are: a) slip them into a woven placemat which can be rolled up and tied with ribbon for storage or travel, b) fasten them to cardboard with elastic or rubber bands, c) stand them on their handle ends in a glass or jar, d) store them in a machine sewn fabric case specially designed to separate the brushes and prevent them from shifting. In the case of the Loew-Cornell kit, the plastic container has ventilation holes so it can be used for brush storage.

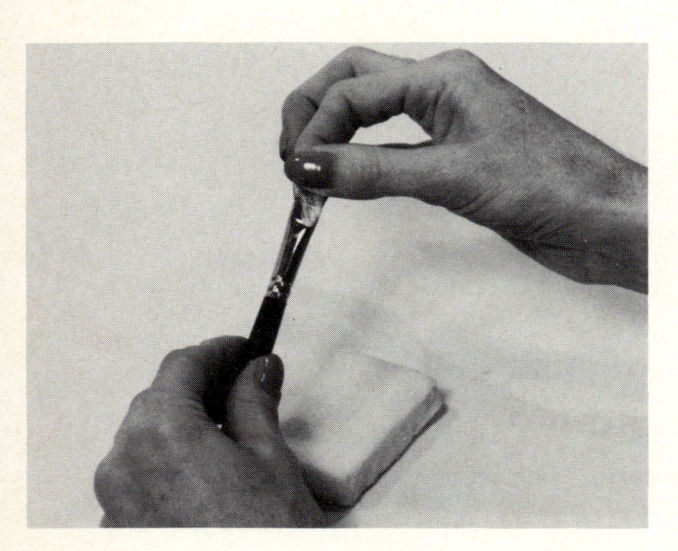

Figure 8. Working soap into the hairs is essential.

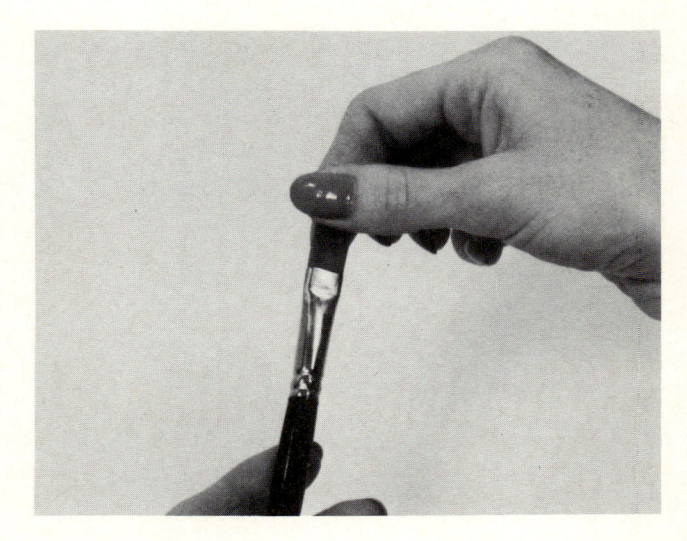

Figure 9. Reshaping the hairs.

Figure 10. Protect your brushes when storing them.

SURFACE PREPARATION

Pictured are six basic steps to follow in preparing wooden projects for decorative painting.

1. Fill holes and flaws with wood putty or wood filler.

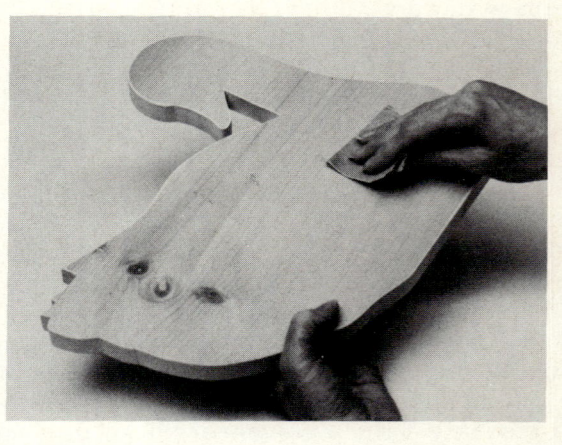

2. Sand, moving with the grain of the wood. If the wood is especially rough, begin sanding with a coarse texture paper. Follow this with a medium texture paper and lastly, with a fine texture.

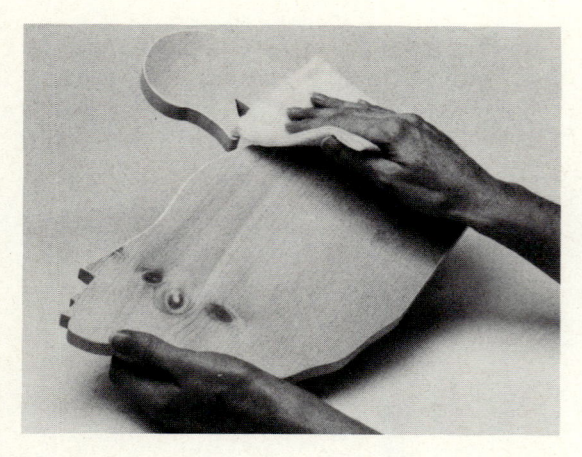

3. Remove dust thoroughly with a tack cloth.

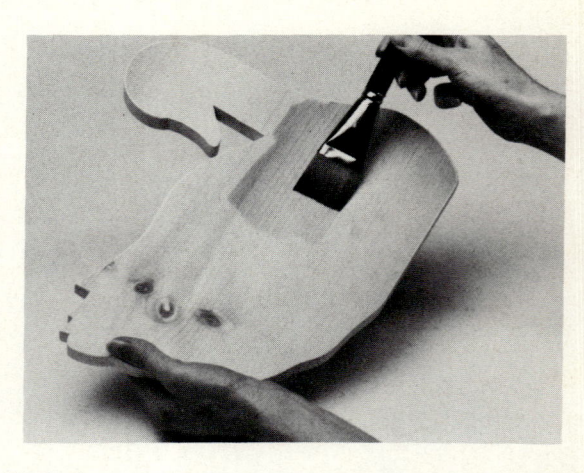

4. Seal the wood with any clear sealer, waterbased varnish, or, preferably, clear shellac. Sealing will raise the grain slightly. Dry, according to manufacturer's instructions.

5. Sand very lightly with fine sandpaper, steel wool, or abrasive "scrubbie." Again, remove all dust with tack cloth.

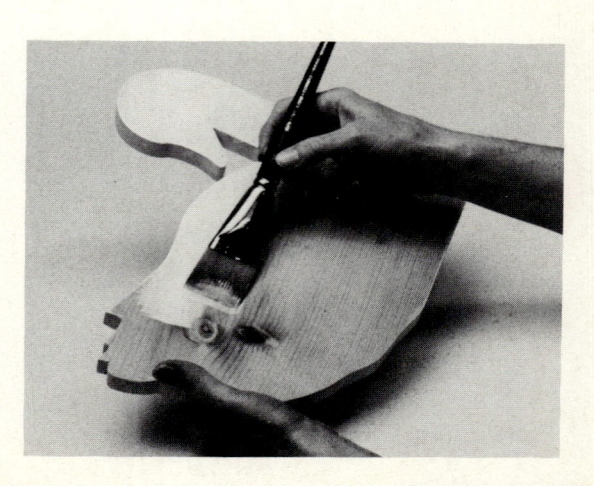

6. Basecoat with background color. Several thin coats are preferable to a thick, uneven one. Sand if necessary with fine textured paper. Surface should feel satiny smooth.

TRANSFERRING PATTERNS

In order for you to develop your greatest potential as a decorative folk artist, it is preferable that you not limit yourself to the rigid confines of a pattern. To do so tends to stifle your creativity. Realizing, however, that there are times when the slight suggestion of a pattern might serve as a "security blanket," I will share the following tips with you. Notice, however, the mention of "slight suggestion." This means that you are encouraged to trace the least amount of pattern possible, leaving as much opportunity as you can for your own personal interpretation and embellishment.

1. Copy the pattern onto tracing paper.

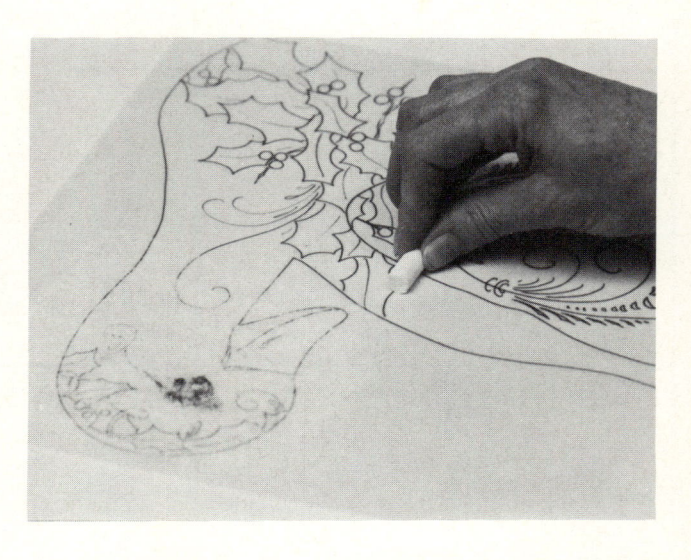

2. Rub chalk on the back of the pattern. Use a color which will barely show against your background and which will not muddy your work. Cheap chalk is best (do not use oil pastels). Shake off excess chalk dust.

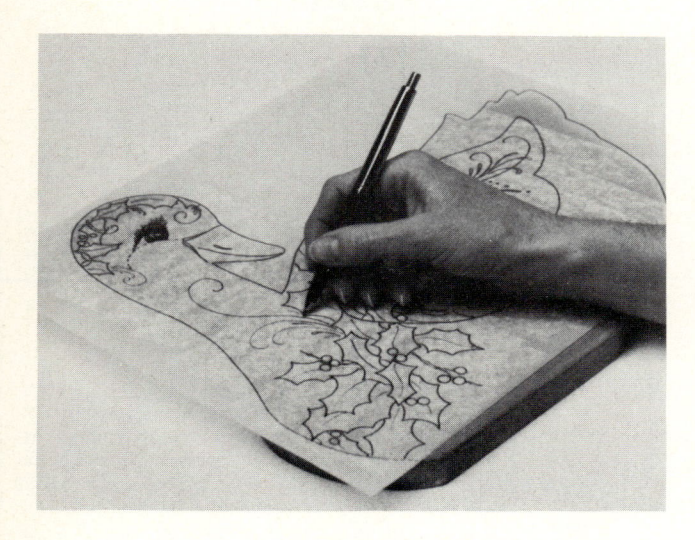

3. Tape pattern in place. Retrace pattern lines. Use a different color pen so you will be able to see where you have retraced. If you plan to use the pattern repeatedly, trace it onto Vidalon or Deluxe Vellum - a sturdier grade of tracing paper. You can protect the tracing by placing a piece of waxed paper over it before transferring it to your project. Retrace your pattern lines through the waxed paper. You will be able to see by the tracks in the waxed paper where you have traced and where you have missed.

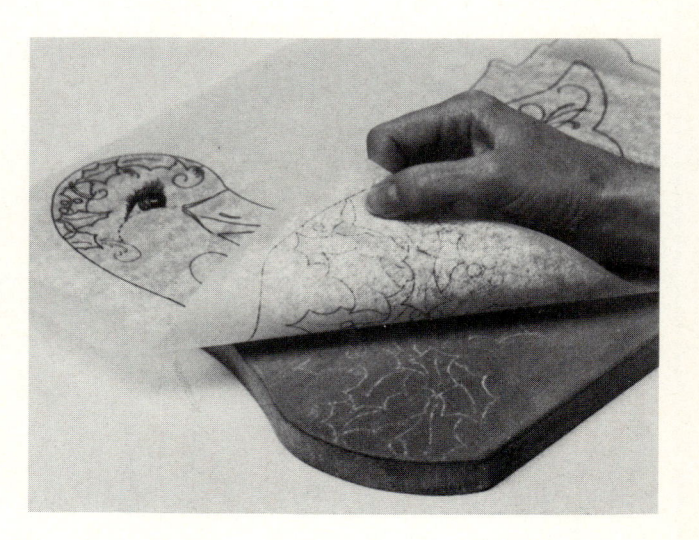

4. Before removing the pattern, lift it carefully to see that all critical parts transferred clearly. The chalked pattern lines wipe away easily with a damp cloth upon completion of your painting.

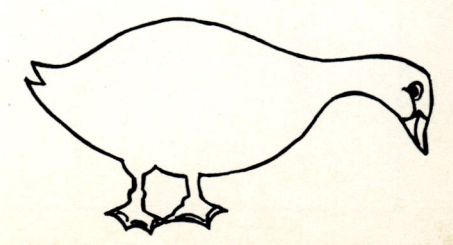

BASIC STROKES FOR FREEHANDING

FLAT BRUSH STROKES

KNIFE STROKE
Slide on the chisel edge of the brush, forming a thin stroke.

BROAD STROKE
Press down the full width of the brush and pull, forming a broad stroke.

Combinations of these two strokes can be used to form the rest of the flat brush strokes.

SCROLL
Begin—on knife edge of brush.
Slide downwards on the knife edge of the brush.
Begin applying pressure as if painting a broad stroke.
Curve gently around.
Begin slowing down and releasing pressure.
Stop. Let hairs return to chisel edge. Lift off.

LEAF STROKE
Begin—as if to paint a broad stroke.
Slowly begin pulling the stroke and rotating the brush simultaneously (by pulling the brush with your thumb) to a 90 degree angle.
End by sliding briefly on the knife edge.

"S"
Begin on the knife edge. Slide.
Gradually reverse directions and apply pressure.
Gradually decrease pressure and reverse directions.
Slide briefly on the knife edge.
Slow down. Let brush hairs return to chisel edge.
Stop. Lift off.

CRESCENT
Begin, sliding very briefly on knife edge.
Apply pressure as for a broad stroke.
Gradually release pressure, letting hairs return to chisel.

RUFFLED CRESCENT
Slide briefly on knife edge.
This stroke is executed like the crescent, except that varying amounts of pressure are applied and released. You'll do this one well with a severe case of hiccups.

FLAT COMMA
This stroke is like the scroll stroke, only done in reverse direction; i.e. begin at fat end, slide to knife edge.

SIDELOADED BRUSH
Color should blend gradually from intense color to a faded wash.
Have a bit of water in your brush to achieve the blend.

DOUBLELOADED BRUSH
Load 2 colors onto the brush, one on either edge.
Stroke the brush on the palette to blend, softening the contrast in the middle.

LINER/ROUND BRUSH STROKES

CROSSHATCH
Use thinned paint and stay on tip of brush

"S"
Begin—follow directions for "S" stroke with flat brush.

CRESCENT
Begin.
Curve, applying gentle pressure.
Apply full pressure in center.
Gradually release pressure.
Slow down, let brush hairs return to point.
Stop. Lift off.

TEARDROP
Begin.
Pull, apply gradual pressure.
More pressure.
Stop. Lift straight up

PIGTAIL TEARDROP
Begin.
This stroke is identical to the teardrop, except after stopping, raise the brush but do not lift off. Leave point in contact. Drag point of brush thru fat head of stroke creating a wiggly tail.

COMMA
Begin—press and pause.
Gradually begin pulling the stroke and releasing pressure.
Slow down, letting hairs return to point.
Stop. Lift off.

CHOCOLATE CHIP
Begin—press a blob. 
Flick the tip of brush thru blob.

SCROLL
Begin—use pressure and release motions from above strokes to paint graceful scrolls.

FINISHING TECHNIQUES

All projects should be given a protective varnish coat once the painted design is dry and all pattern lines or chalk guidelines have been removed. Here's how:

BRUSH ON VARNISH

1. Ideally, varnishing should be done in a warm, dust free room without moving air (good luck!).
2. Varnish (any satin finish variety) and object should be 72 degrees or more. Cold varnish has a tendency to "crawl" away from the surface.
3. Apply varnish in fair weather to facilitate proper drying (which for many oil based varnishes is 24 hours or more). Humid weather slows the drying process. For waterbased varnish, drying time is usually just a matter of minutes.
4. Before varnishing, remove dust from object by wiping with a tack cloth. You can buy one or make it yourself. Dip a 12" square of cheesecloth in warm water. Wring out excess. Mix 2 teaspoons turpentine with 3 teaspoons varnish. Pour over the cloth and work into it. Store in airtight container.
5. Do not shake varnish. To do so causes unwanted bubbles. However, varnish should be thoroughly stirred to distribute the drying agent.
6. Never use old, thick varnish, and do not attempt to thin it for use. Such varnish would result in a disappointing finish. Throw it away.
7. Try to "flow" varnish on smoothly with a good quality varnish brush. I prefer Loew-Cornell's Series 7550, 1½" brush. Avoid wiping brush on lip of can, and do not brush excessively. Both actions cause bubbles.
8. As you apply varnish, check edges to be sure varnish is not building up (the action of passing the brush over an edge wrings a little extra varnish out). Wipe any excess off or smooth with the brush.
9. Place in a dust and draft free area to dry thoroughly. Drying a surface horizontally will keep the varnish from sagging. Be sure to place a cover a few inches above the surface to protect it from dust.
10. Wipe with the tack cloth, then apply a second coat of varnish and let dry thoroughly.
11. With #600 wet and dry sandpaper sprinkled with water and a little liquid soap to reduce friction, or with #0000 steel wool, or with an abrasive sponge, sand **very lightly** after the second and any successive coats of varnish except the last one. Rinse off soap. Dry. Tack and varnish again, building up as many coats as desired. (For something which will hang on the wall, 3 coats of finish are usually sufficient. For heavy use items, I will often use ten or more coats.)

FOR A HAND RUBBED FINISHED (Optional)

After the last coat of varnish, dry 48 hours. Sprinkle surface with powdered pumice (4F dental grade is available from your drug store) or rottenstone (even finer than pumice), and a little finishing oil (baby oil, linseed oil, or lemon oil will suffice). Then rub gently using the palm of your hand or a scrap of heavy felt to produce a satin finish. Buff with a soft, clean, dry cloth.

On some pieces a quicker finishing process may be adequate. Simply buff the piece with a well worn, crumpled brown paper grocery bag.

SPRAY VARNISH

1. If you prefer to use spray varnish, carefully follow the manufacturer's directions on the can. With some sprays, it is necessary to apply successive coats within a certain period of time to prevent crinkling of the finish.
2. Never combine different types of varnishes. Chemical incompatibilities often lead to disastrous results.
3. Varnish and project should be at room temperature. The first four principles listed above for brush on varnish also apply to spray varnish.
4. Test the spray on a scrap to assure the spray head is clean and operating properly.
5. Spray your project by beginning the spray off the edge, then sweeping across the project all the way to the other side and off the edge. This prevents drippy buildup at the beginning and ending points.
6. Spray lightly. Several thin coats are preferable to one heavy coat. Heavy spraying results in blobs and drips.
7. It is possible to give a hand rubbed finish to sprayed pieces in the same manner as for brush on varnish. Be careful to sand carefully. The sprayed on varnish coat will be much thinner than one that has been brushed on and could easily be sanded through to the paint underneath.

HINTS

1. Finish the back of your project, removing any paint and varnish drips. Stain, paint or cover the back with wallpaper samples.
2. Pull-tabs from soda cans make handy hanging hooks, or use sawtooth hangers. Be sure to nail hangers in place before assembling dimensional items on the front of your project.
3. For a weatherproof finish, use a marine spar varnish.
4. Heat and alcohol-proof varnishes are ideal for trays and heavy use items.
5. Project pieces which are to be glued together bond more securely if sealer, paint, and varnish are not applied to the area to be glued. A piece of drafting tape placed over the area to be glued while working will protect it. Remove the tape before gluing.

See page 21 for instructions on antiquing/glazing.

JACKIE'S GOLDEN GOOSE

The Golden Goose was the first project conceived and executed for this book, thus, the book's name. The goose was designed as a Christmas centerpiece to be ringed with fresh holly. It is shown in color on page 19.

The Golden Goose is also the most time consuming project in the book because of the gold leafing. The leaf may be ommitted if you prefer and the goose painted with Camel and Taffy using a natural sponge to dab on the colors. The resulting parchment color is striking against the bold holly leaves.

Materials

Goose cutout
Gold leaf size
Gold leaf - approximately 13 sheets
Gold leaf sealer
Chalk
Acrylic paints:

Rusty Nail	Sunny Yellow	Thicket
Shamrock	Raspberry Wine	Lemonade
Wrought Iron	Autumn Leaves	Primrose
Fresh Foliage	Coffee Bean	Taffy
Moon Glow	Cinnamon	

Brushes:
  ½", #2, #4, #6, and #10 flats
  Jackie's Liner #2

Directions

PREPARING THE SURFACE

Follow steps 1-6 of general surface preparation on page 8. Leave a silver dollar sized patch under each wing unsealed so that the wedge which holds the wings away from the body may be glued to raw wood for better adhesion. Basecoat entire goose (except for the silver dollar sized patch under each wing) with Rusty Nail. When dry, rub smooth with a crumpled paper bag. Wipe with a tack cloth.

DESIGNING THE PATTERN

Use chalk to freehand sketch a holly garland around the goose's neck and head. Also, sketch 5 or 6 leaves onto each wing. Use the pattern as a guide, but don't worry about exact reproduction. You can hardly go wrong with holly. (Or, if you prefer, trace on the pattern, following directions on page 9.)

APPLYING GOLD LEAF

Apply gold leaf size following manufacturer's directions. (Or use a resin-type varnish such as McCloskey's Heirloom.) Let size or varnish dry to the tacky stage. Test for "doneness" by touching a knuckle of your finger to it. When you remove your knuckle it should feel and sound as if you were removing it from cellophane tape. When the proper tack stage has been reached, apply gold leaf. Unless you are quite wealthy or extravagant, you will most likely be using imitation or Dutch gold leaf. Avoid handling the leaf with your fingers. Lift leaf out of the package by using a large soft brush or a 6" square of waxed paper or plastic. Rub brush, paper or plastic lightly on your hair to create static electricity which will enable you to lift the leaf. Move the leaf to the tacky surface and lay it in place. Use the brush to pat leaf gently against size, shaping it around edges where necessary.

Leaf entire project in this manner, always being sure to remove leaves from package in the same direction. (Often one side of the leaves in the package will vary slightly in color from the other side.) Use scraps to mend gaps and large cracks. The smaller hairline cracks which appear lend an air of antiquity to the piece as, traditionally, leaf was applied over a red clay base. Follow leaf and size manufacturers' directions for drying times, then burnish with soft cotton balls. Apply gold leaf sealer or a coat of varnish to protect the leaf and prevent the imitation leaf from tarnishing. Preferring a well-worn, time-aged look, I handle the piece rather roughly after reaching this point, letting edges rub and wear through the thin protective coat of sealer, thus permitting the Rusty Nail background to show through.

Continued on page 15

Dashed line indicates approximate location of wooden wedge which allows wing to flare about 1½" away from body.

Use this pattern only as a guide. Add leaves wherever needed. Be sure to carry the design over the edges.

HOLLY

BLENDING TECHNIQUES

1. Basecoat leaf with Thicket. Dry.

2. Apply a second basecoat of Thicket, picking up a little Shamrock and applying it randomly to provide color variations. Add Wrought Iron in center and at base of leaf.

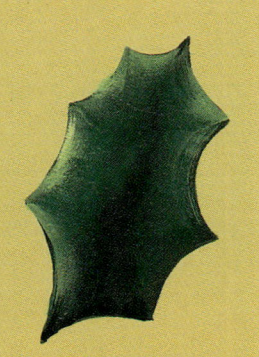

3. Highlight with Fresh Foliage by sideloading, doubleloading, or drybrushing.

Sideloaded brush

Doubleloaded brush

Drybrush

4. Sideload brush with Wrought Iron. Paint an "S" stroke through the center of the leaf.

5. Mix Fresh Foliage with Moonglow and water. Use the liner to paint veins and stickers.

BERRIES

1. Basecoat with Rusty Nail.

2. Shade with Raspberry Wine.

3. Highlight with Primrose plus Autumn Leaves.

4. Add a small stroke of reflected light (Primrose plus Autumn Leaves) beneath the shading.

5. Add a small intense spot of highlight with Autumn Leaves plus Lemonade.

PAINTING THE DESIGN

Holly

Basecoat all holly leaves with Thicket, using the #4 flat on large leaves, and the #2 flat on small leaves on the head. Apply a second coat of Thicket, picking up a little Shamrock periodically, and at times, Shamrock plus Wrought Iron. Use the Shamrock/Wrought Iron mixture primarily at the base of leaves, in the centers, and in shadow areas.

Highlight the leaves (generally on the edges) with Fresh Foliage. For stronger highlights, add a little Moon Glow to the Fresh Foliage. Here are four methods for highlighting:

1. **Sideload** the brush with a thin wash of color, floating the lights on over the dry base coat.
2. **Doubleload** the brush with the highlight color on one side and Thicket, or Thicket plus Shamrock, on the other side and working over a dry basecoat.
3. Use either method 1 or 2 above and work right into wet basecoat.
4. **Drybrush**, by loading the flat brush with color, then wiping as much as possible from the brush. The scant paint remaining in the brush is lightly skimmed across surface to be highlighted (See color worksheet on holly on page 14 and on bows on page 27.)

I use all four methods; however, you may find you prefer one technique over the others.

Caution: Do not overwork the blending. Overblended colors lose their pizazz and their individual character. Also, do not attempt to exactly duplicate each leaf as shown on the painted sample—that's too frustrating. Instead, concentrate on working at least 3-4 values (lights and darks) into each leaf.

Paint a thinned sideloaded Wrought Iron "S" stroke in the center of the leaf. Mix Fresh Foliage plus Sunny Yellow, plus water and use the liner to paint a very thin line along the darkest side of the "S" stroke. Then paint vein lines, curving them to help suggest contours of the leaf. Keep the vein lines almost obscure. See color worksheet on page 14.

Berries

Basecoat berries with Rusty Nail. Shade the lower side with a crescent stroke of Raspberry Wine. Highlight top with thinned Primrose plus Autumn Leaves. Use the liner and add a thin crescent stroke of Primrose/Autumn Leaves mixture to apply a reflected highlight or secondary highlight near the bottom of the berry. Dry. Add a smaller, more intense highlight on the top of the berry with Autumn Leaves plus Lemonade. Apply shadows beneath the berry with a thin wash of Wrought Iron on #2 flat.

Stems

Though very few stems are obvious, paint them with Coffee Bean. Use Wrought Iron to shade or strengthen color.

Scroll Work

Use the liner and Rusty Nail plus Raspberry Wine. On the wings, in addition to the red scrollwork, add green scrolls and strokes using Thicket plus Fresh Foliage.

Beak

Apply a thin wash of Autumn Leaves with the #10 flat. Dry. Shade with Rusty Nail, beginning at the base of the beak. While wet, wipe out a highlight along the edge of the top beak by sliding the rinsed out, damp #10 flat along the beak from base to tip. Shade beneath the wiped-out line with Rusty Nail plus Coffee Bean. Outline beak with Coffee Bean comma strokes. Add a smaller Coffee Bean comma stroke on the beak for a "nostril."

Cheek

With the #10 flat, apply a thin wash of Primrose. Dry. Sideload the brush with Cinnamon. Blend into cheek placing intense color side of brush to the top of the cheek. Dry. Mix a little Cinnamon with Taffy. Use the #4 flat to drybrush highlights on the cheek.

Eye

Using #4 flat, fill in eye shape with Taffy. Shade corner with Wrought Iron (this is optional, and is not shown on the color worksheet on page 36). Dry. Paint the iris Fresh Foliage. While wet, paint pupil Thicket. Dry. Deepen pupil with Wrought Iron. Shade top of iris with Thicket. Highlight eye with Moon Glow. Outline the eye and form lashes with liner and Coffee Bean. Deepen lash color if necessary with Wrought Iron. See the color worksheet mentioned above for step by step method of painting simple eyes.

Finishing

Wipe away all chalk marks. Apply one coat of varnish.

Antiquing

Use a soft cloth (cheese cloth) to apply antiquing glaze sparingly. (See page 21 for tips on antiquing.) The goose was antiqued with a glaze of Burnt Umber plus Raw Sienna.

Varnishing

Let antiquing dry thoroughly and cure several days before applying final coats of varnish. (See page 11 for instructions on varnishing.)

FAMILY "WEATHERVANE"

This was my favorite project to work on simply because I love to do things which involve, or remind me of, my family.

*"The supreme happiness of life
Is the conviction that we are loved."*

That lovely sentiment from Hugo is lettered around the outside edge of the large heart (which also bears our family name). You may have other quotations or verses which are significant to your family, and which could be lettered in the large heart or along the length of the narrow strip. The smaller heart contains Lynn's and my names and our wedding date. Along the narrow strip, there is a different goose for each family member accompanied by first and middle names, and date of birth.

Materials

Geese cutouts—one for each member of the family
Large heart 6" x 6", small heart 3½" x 4" (Patterns are superimposed on this page)
Narrow strip of wood 1½" x 33" (more or less, depending upon size of family)
Acrylic Paints:
   Taffy   Persimmon
   Harvest Gold Patchwork Green
   Rusty Nail   Wrought Iron
   Promenade
Brushes:
   #4 flat
   Jackie's Liner #2
Ribbon ⅛" x 4" for each goose
Glue
Drafting tape

Directions

1. Before sealing or painting, place hearts and geese along strip in desired positions. Outline each with chalk or lightly with a pencil. Remove cutouts and within the outlined area place a piece of drafting tape approximately ¾" long. The tape will prevent sealer and paint from soaking into the covered area and thus allow better bonding of the cutouts with glue upon assembly.

2. Prepare the individual pieces for decorating by sealing, sanding, and basecoating. Basecoat the hearts and narrow strip Rusty Nail (or whatever color best suits your decor). Basecoat the geese (beaks and feet included) Taffy. Apply a second coat if necessary for good coverage. Be sure to paint all edges, too. (If you paint the backs, leave the lower portion unpainted for good glue adhesion.)

3. BEAKS and FEET. Use the #4 flat to paint beaks and feet Persimmon thinned slightly with water. Shade webs in feet and base of beaks with Rusty Nail.

4. CHEEKS. Paint cheeks Promenade with a #4 flat. Add a Taffy highlight.

5. EYES. With the liner, paint eyes Patchwork Green. Add Wrought Iron pupils and Taffy highlights.

6. Use the liner and Harvest Gold to paint assorted detail strokes ("S", comma, scroll, etc.) to represent wings.

7. Reposition the cutouts to determine spacing for names and dates. Draw chalk lines to help keep letters even. Use the liner and thinned Taffy to do the lettering. Embellish with detail strokes of Taffy and Harvest Gold.

8. Varnish all pieces.
9. Remove tape and glue all pieces into place.
10. Hang and enjoy!

17

GRAPEVINE WREATH WITH GOBBLING GANDERS

Since popped corn is the most important, most consistent, and most favorite food item here at the Old Stone Mill, it seemed highly appropriate that it should be commemorated in a wreath. The partial ear of popping corn is some which we raised at the mill. The wreath is shown in color on page 19.

Materials

18″ grapevine wreath
Bow
Cornhusk doll (available in craft stores)
3 geese cutouts (approx. 3½″)
Ear of popping corn or loose kernels
Popsicle stick
Glue
Wood thimble
Thin wire, 3″
Acrylic Paints:
    Taffy   Rusty Nail
    Promenade   Nutmeg
    Wicker White Patchwork Green
    Persimmon
Brushes:
    #4 and #10 flats
    Jackie's Liner #2

Directions

1. Paint geese cutouts as described for "Family Weathervane" on page 16. Use the Wicker White for strokes on the wings. (Or, if you prefer more contrast, use Harvest Gold.) Paint space between feet (if necessary) with Nutmeg.

2. Paint dress of cornhusk doll and her thimble pail in colors to match bow. (Note: directions for making your own bow can be found in "Christmas at The Old Stone Mill.")

3. Drill tiny holes in the thimble to insert wire for a handle. Fill the thimble pail with kernels of popcorn and glue in place. Hang on doll's arm.

4. Place glue on one end of popsicle stick and insert in bottom of doll's dress. Weave other end among gravevines and glue, being certain doll is standing straight.

5. Glue the corn and loose kernels in place.

6. Varnish the geese. When dry, glue them in position around the corn.

Note: Use quick setting glue such as Tacky Glue or a hot glue gun for easier handling of the pieces.

POPCORN CANNISTER

Here is another quick, easy, inexpensive idea to use for gifts or bazaar items. Decorate a couple of geese cutouts as described in the "Family Weathervane" on page 16. These geese were embellished with Rusty Nail strokes for wings, and red ribbons. Glue them to a New Berlin Plastics Country Keeper cannister (or a large glass jar or glass cannister). Glue the lid ring to the plastic lid with Dow Corning Silicone Rubber Clear Adhesive. When dry, flood the lid with Envirotex (available at craft stores), totally embedding the kernels. The cannister is shown in color on page 19.

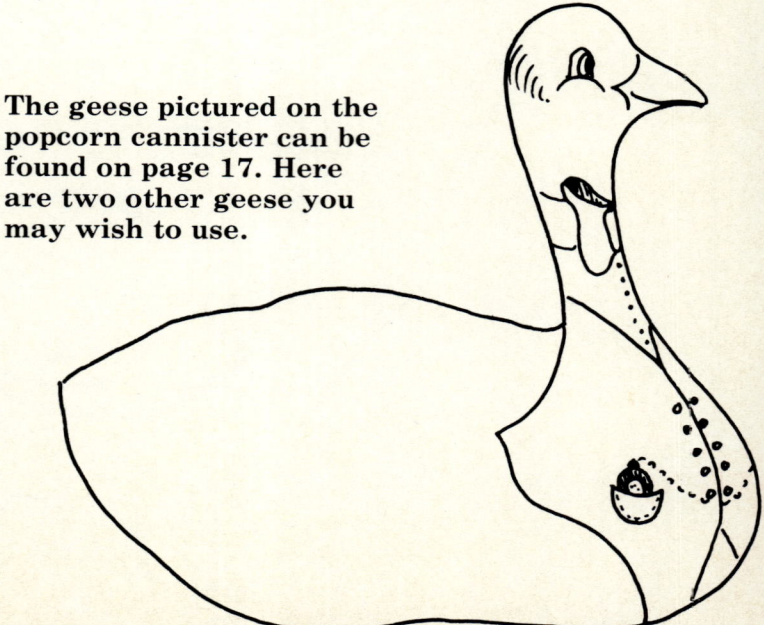

The geese pictured on the popcorn cannister can be found on page 17. Here are two other geese you may wish to use.

19

"SLATS" GOOSE TOTE

The wood in this tote was too pretty to cover with paint, so I left it natural and used thin washes of color for the goose's face and scarf.

Materials

"Slats" Goose Tote
   11½" high x 15" x 18"
Acrylic Paints:
   Promenade
   Persimmon
   Slate Blue
   Wicker White
   Licorice
   Sunny Yellow
   Harvest Gold
   Nutmeg
Brushes:
   #6, ½" flats
   Jackie's Liner #2

Procedure

1. Seal entire tote. Dry. Sand lightly. Wipe away dust with a tack cloth. Seal again. Dry, sand, and remove dust.

2. Paint Promenade cheeks with a sideloaded ½" flat brush. Add Wicker White teardrops for highlights.

3. Sideload the #6 flat brush with Persimmon to paint the beak. Outline the beak with Nutmeg.

4. With the #6 flat brush, fill in the eyes with Wicker White. Paint the iris Slate Blue and the pupil Licorice. Add Wicker White highlights. Outline the eye, then shade above it with a thin wash of Nutmeg.

5. Use Harvest Gold and Sunny Yellow on the liner to paint oodles of comma strokes and/or teardrops to form hair, eyelashes, and wings.

6. Apply a thin wash of Slate Blue to the scarf with the ½" flat brush. Use some Slate Blue sideloaded on the brush to suggest folds in the fabric.

7. Decorate the scarf with colors already used in the rest of the project. Or, coordinate all colors to match your own fabric lining for the tote.

8. Apply several coats of protective varnish to the tote. (See Finishing Techniques, page 11.)

Continued from page 11

ANTIQUING/GLAZING

Some projects lend themselves nicely to antiquing or glazing. Use this technique as an enhancing measure only on those projects which are appropriate or would benefit from it. It is neither necessary nor desirable to get into the habit of antiquing everything you paint.

To antique a project, you will need a clear glaze (see recipe below), oil paints, palette knife, palette, cheesecloth, a mop brush, a sponge brush, and extra fine steel wool or a Home and Hobby Pad ("scrubby"). Plastic or rubber gloves are advisable as this technique tends to be a bit messy. (Lacking gloves, slip your hands into a couple of sandwich baggies.)

Mix a clear glaze medium as follows:

1 tablespoon varnish (I use McCloskey's)
3 tablespoons paint thinner or turpentine (dirty turp is great)
1-2 drops linseed oil

Proportions of the recipe may be varied to suit your preferences. (More turpentine makes the glaze thinner. More varnish accelerates the drying time. More linseed oil retards the drying time.) Frequently, if I am out of my glaze, I will use the palette knife to scoop small amounts of the ingredients onto my palette - no calculated measurements - just rough proportions.

Select a color of oil paint to be mixed with the glaze. Gradually add glaze to the oil paint until the mixture is workable, but still fairly dense. Popular oil paint colors to use for antiquing include Burnt Umber, Raw Umber, Black, Prussian Blue, Burnt Sienna, Raw Sienna. These colors may be used individually or in mixtures. It is a good idea to make a test sample of your design colors for the purpose of experimenting to see which antiquing color or combination of colors you prefer over the designs.

It is also possible to glaze with other colors - such as red, yellow, green, etc. In such a case, the effect is not so much one of antiquity as it is an interesting treatment of color.

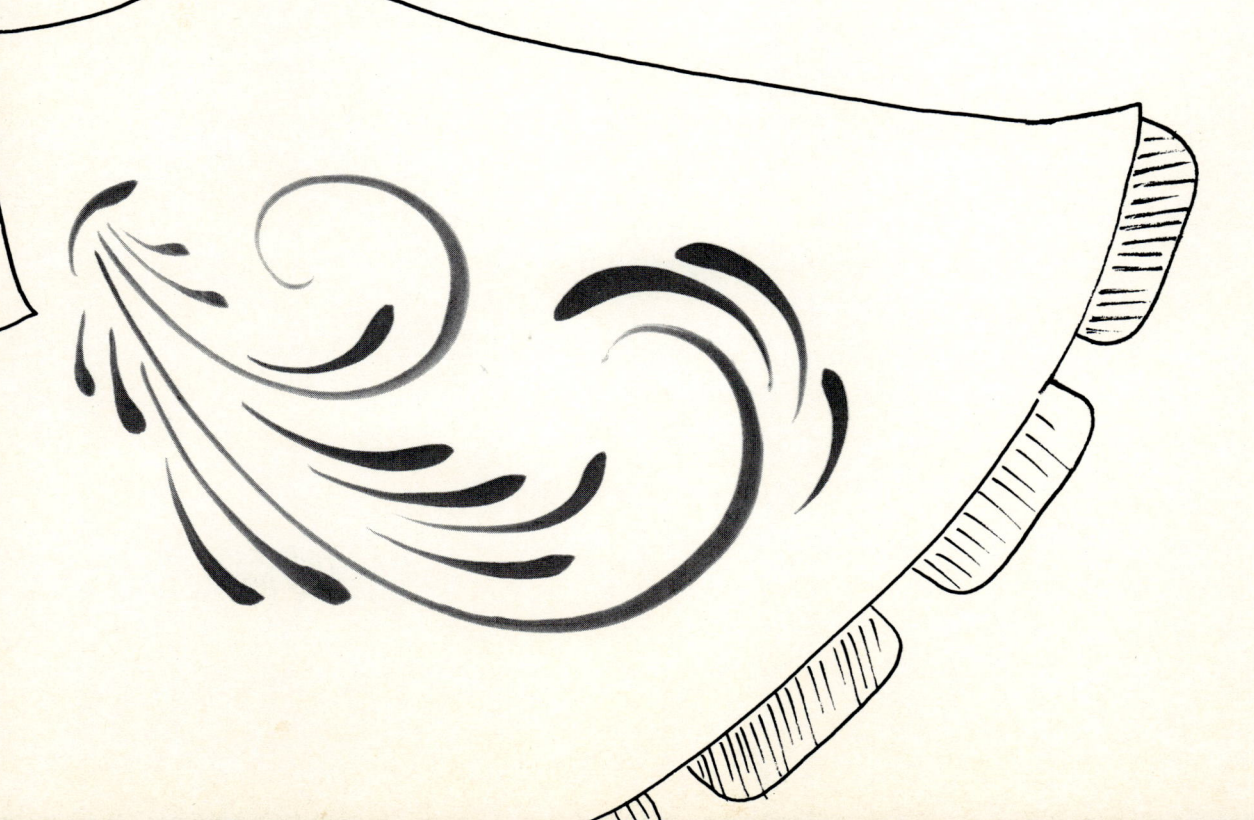

22

THE SPRUCE GOOSE

A bit of capriciousness set in as I began working on the flying goose. His name comes from Howard Hughes' giant wooden plane. The flying goggles, scarf, and wing insignia then came naturally. The little boy in your family (be he young or old) may have his own ideas for "sprucing up" this goose. The Spruce Goose can hang from the ceiling or be mounted on a dowel and stand. He is shown in color on page 22.

Materials

Wooden flying goose: wing 15", body 7" x 24"
Acrylic Paints:
   Taffy   Nutmeg
   Persimmon   Thicket
   Rusty Nail   Harvest Gold
   Promenade   Robin's Egg
   Patchwork Green Extender
Brushes:
   #4 and #12 flats
   Jackie's Liner #2
Heavy nylon fishing line
Plastic wrap
Glue
Masking tape
Eye screw

Directions

1. Determine positions of wings and feet. Cover the areas to be glued with masking tape to facilitate stronger bonding of the glue after decoration is complete. Basecoat goose body, feet, and wings Taffy.

2. BEAK. Paint beak with a thin wash of Persimmon letting Taffy basecoat shine through. Shade base of beak and lower beak with Rusty Nail. Add a Nutmeg comma stroke with the liner.

3. CHEEKS. Sideload the #12 flat with Persimmon and paint the cheeks as illustrated on page 36.

4. EYES. Use Patchwork Green and Thicket, and paint the eyes as illustrated on page 36.

5. GOGGLES. Create a leather-like or mottled texture by pressing crumpled plastic wrap onto painted goggles while they are still wet. Paint the goggles with a thin mixture of Nutmeg and Extender, using the #4 flat. Carefully press the crumbled plastic into the paint and lift, using a fresh section for each pressing.

6. TAIL FEATHERS, BANGS, and WING FEATHERS. Load the liner with Harvest Gold slightly thinned with water. Paint comma strokes for tail and bangs. Paint long flowing scrolls and assorted other detail strokes for the wings.

7. WING INSIGNIA. Using #4 flat, paint the bars Promenade. Paint the circle shape Robin's Egg and outline it with tiny Robin's Egg comma strokes. Add a Taffy star to the middle of the circle. Decorate it with Promenade strokes and dots. Add a few Taffy comma strokes to the bars.

8. FEET. Using #12 flat, paint feet Persimmon, shade webs and wrinkles in legs with Rusty Nail.

9. Varnish all pieces.

10. Remove pieces of masking tape. Glue legs and wings in place.

11. Attach eye screw to upper center back if goose is to hang. Tie a length of heavy nylon fishing line to the eye screw. (Note: if you prefer to have the flying goose as a weathervane, drill a hole in the base and mount on a dowel and stand.)

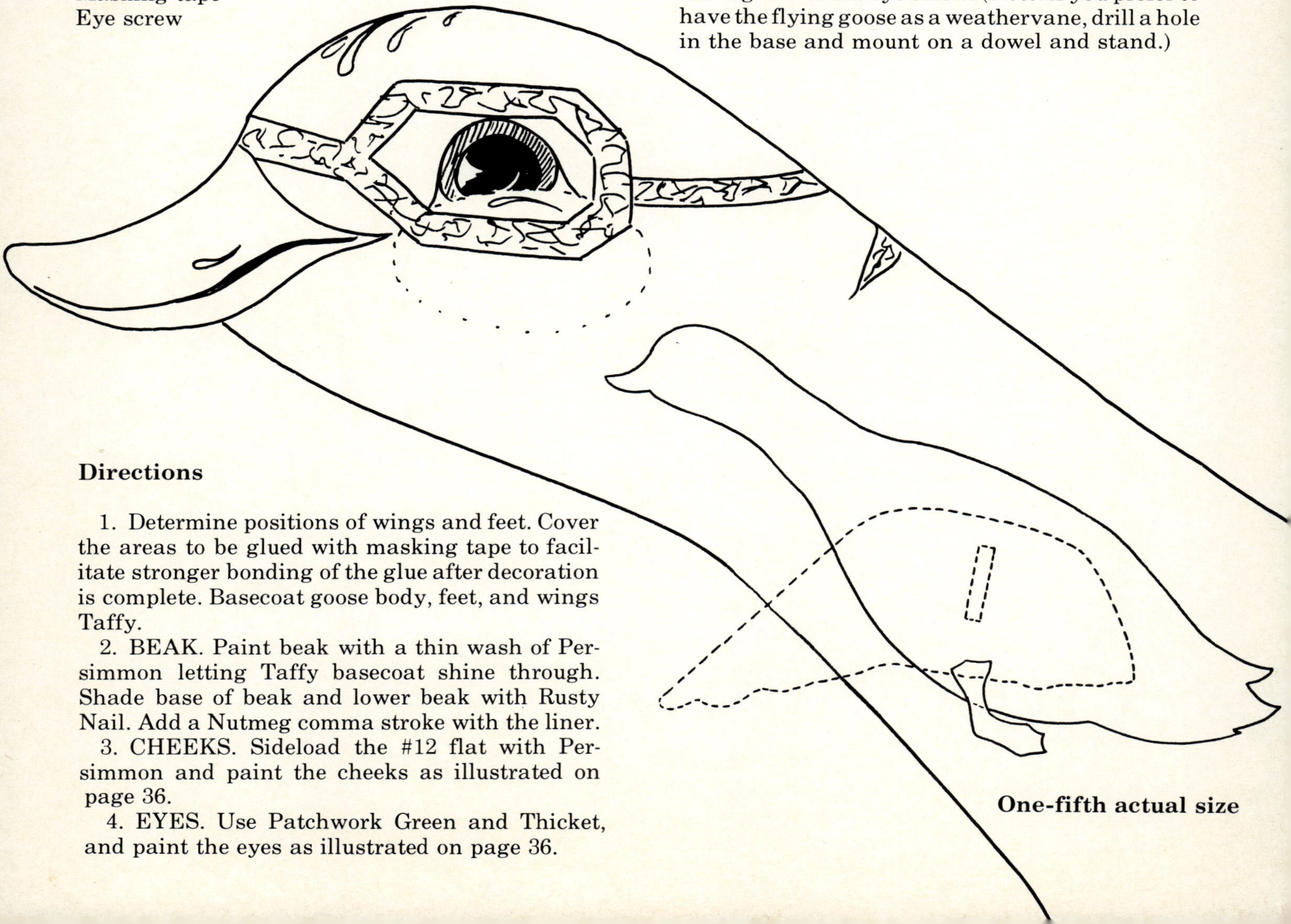

One-fifth actual size

24

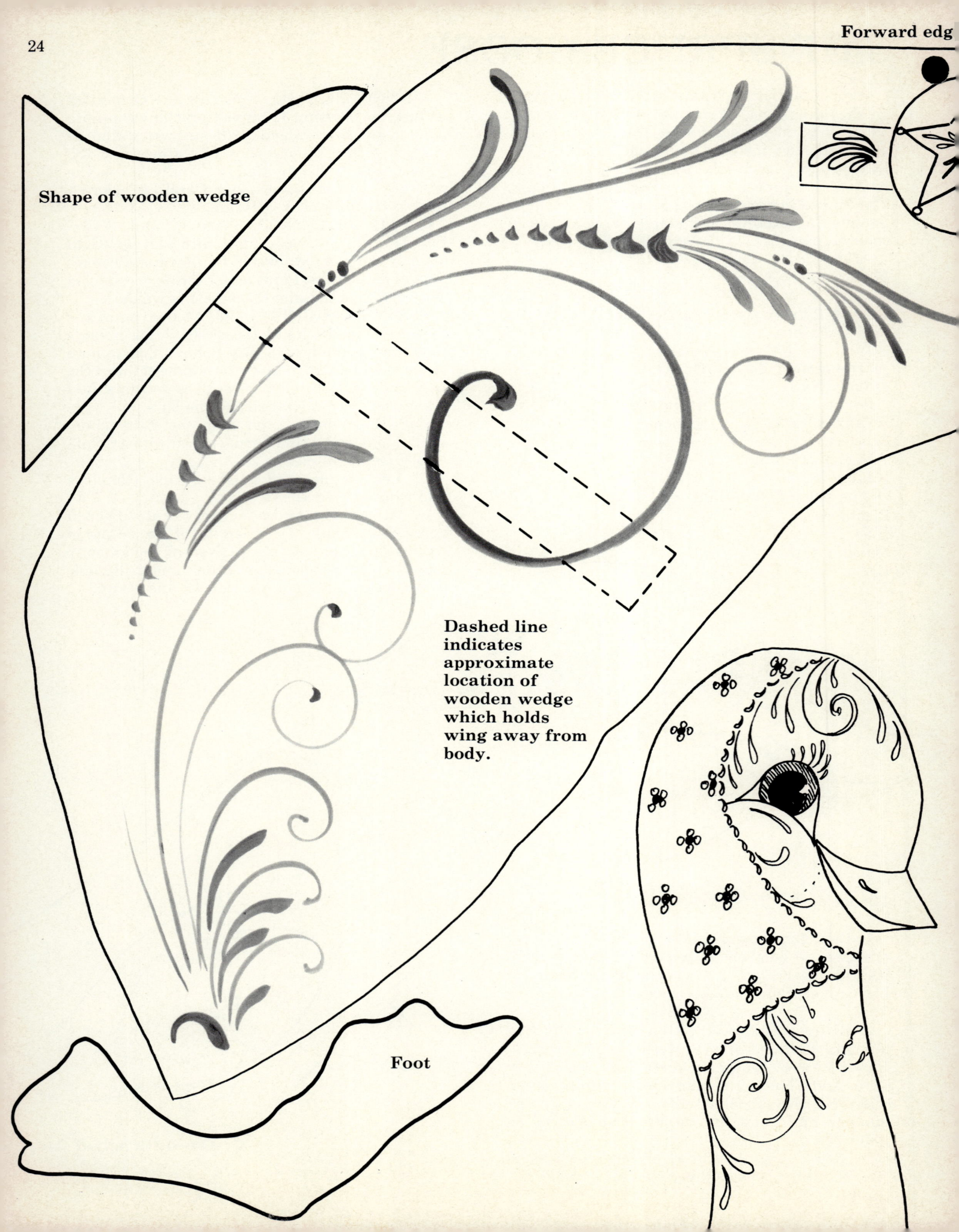

Forward edge

Shape of wooden wedge

Dashed line indicates approximate location of wooden wedge which holds wing away from body.

Foot

LUCKY AND LUCY GOOSEY

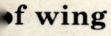

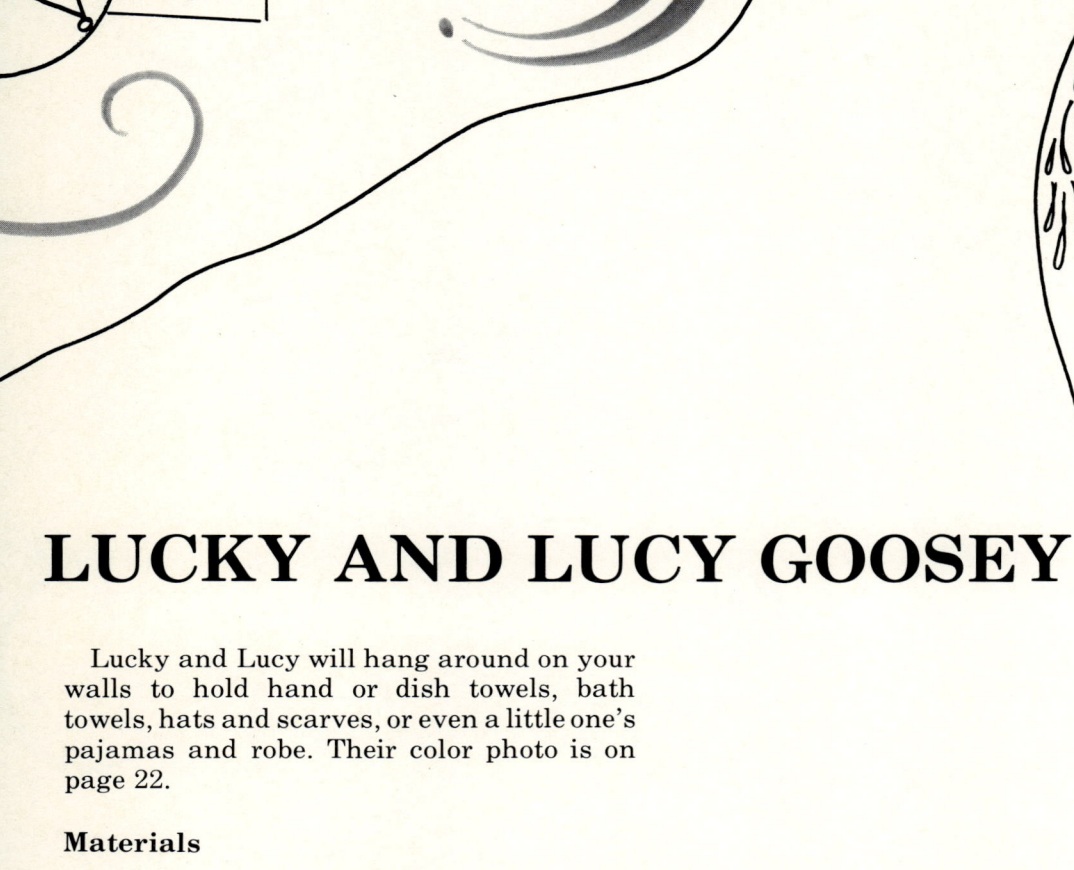

Lucky and Lucy will hang around on your walls to hold hand or dish towels, bath towels, hats and scarves, or even a little one's pajamas and robe. Their color photo is on page 22.

Materials

Wood towel holders 9½" x 9½"
Acrylic Paints:
    Taffy   Wicker White
    Harvest Gold   Persimmon
    Summer Sky   Rusty Nail
    Indigo   Promenade
    Bluegrass   Nutmeg
Brushes:
  #8 flat
  Jackie's Liner #2

Directions

1. Basecoat with Taffy, then follow the general directions for cheeks, beaks, and eyes shown on color worksheet on page 36. Use Bluegrass, Indigo and Wicker White for the eyes. Use Promenade for the cheeks.
2. LUCY'S SCARF and LUCKY'S HAT. Paint a Summer Sky scarf on Lucy and hat on Lucky using #8 flat. Shade each with Indigo. Add Indigo and Wicker White dots and strokes for embellishments.
3. HAIR. Use Harvest Gold strokes and the liner for hair and to paint the scrolls to represent wings.

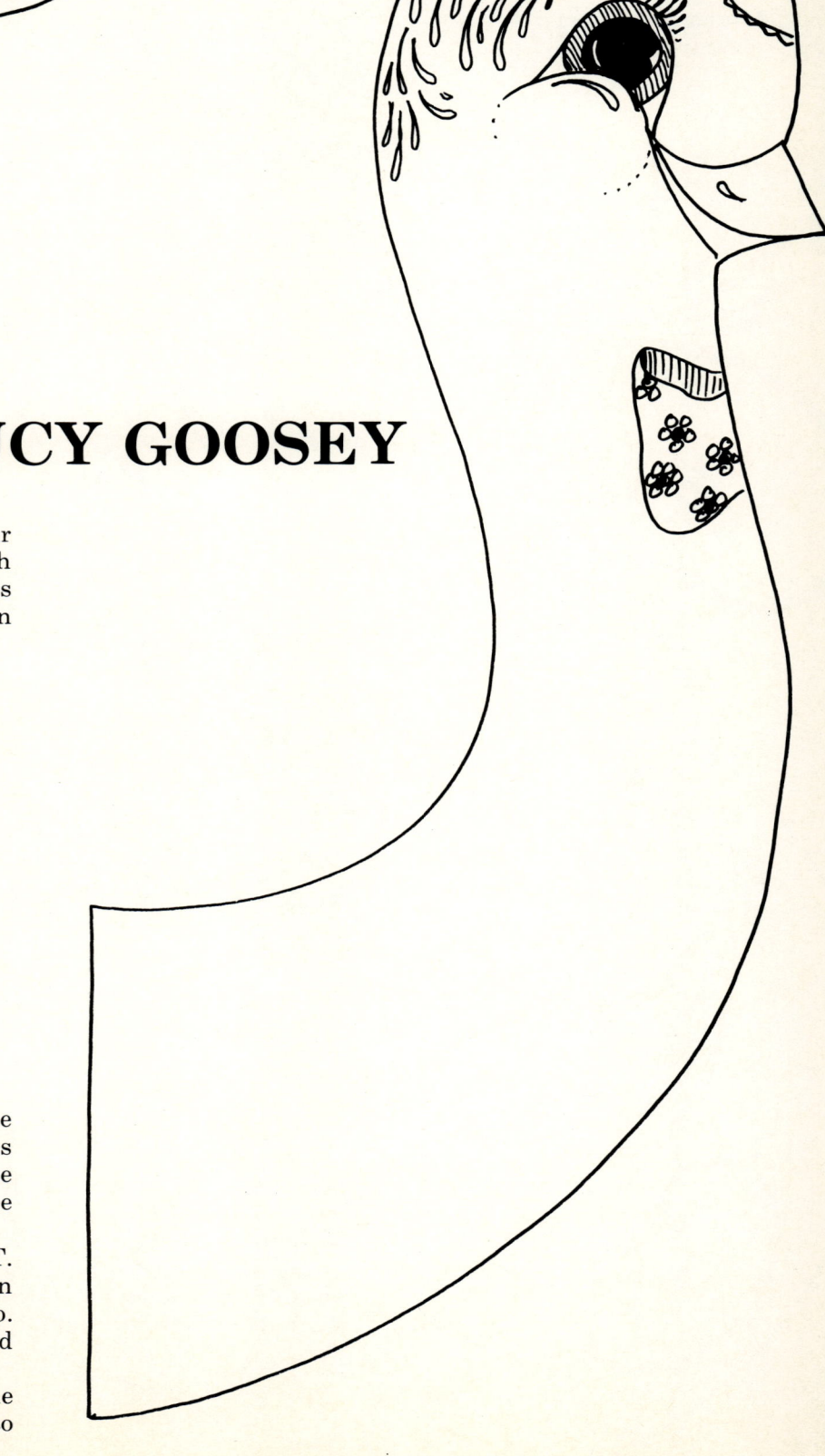

Heart Background for Lucky and Lucy

Alternate pattern for top of heart

To firmly mount head, drill two holes in heart as shown. Carefully drill pilot holes into neck to match. Then screw neck on from the back of heart.

●QUICKIE ROSES

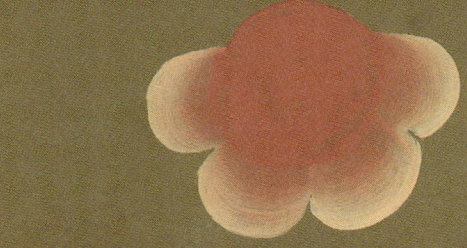

1. Begin with a ball.
2. Add crescent strokes around sides.
3. Add crescent stroke on right of ball.
4. Add "S" stroke on left.

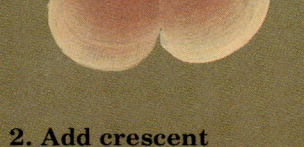

TULIPS

1. Begin with an "S" stroke.
2. Add another "S" facing the other direction.
3. Add optional side and center strokes.
4. Embellish with liner.

FORGET ME NOTS

1. Paint tiny crescent stroke of doubleloaded color.
2. Add four more strokes.
3. Add center dots.

BACKGROUND TECHNIQUES

Sponging

Marbleizing

BOWS

1. Basecoat medium and dark value areas.
2. Add shading under knot and near, but not on, outside edges of bow. Shading, using a sideloaded or doubleloaded brush, may be applied over a wet or dry surface.
3. Add highlights. Dry brush was used here.

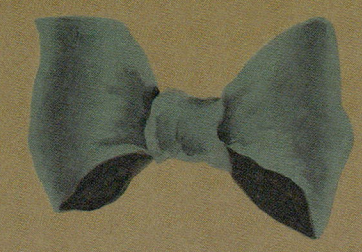

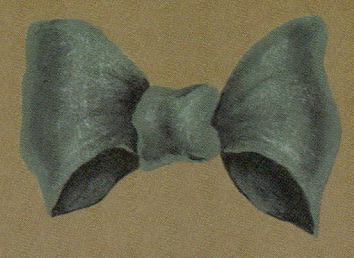

FIVE-DRAWER CHEST

Shown here are half patterns for each of the symmetrically painted drawers. Detailed painting instructions are on page 30. The tin panel insert for the door is punched in the same manner as the tin pie pan described on page 37. The tin punch pattern is on page 3. A color picture of the chest is on page 29.